After Day One

Implementing the Changes in Library of Congress Cataloging

Richard R. Daly
Head, Catalog Department
Swarthmore College Library

American Library Association
Chicago 1981

ISBN: 8389-0338-X

Printed in the United States of America

Contents

Introduction

Many if not most libraries in the United States rely on the Library of Congress (LC) for a significant amount of their cataloging. Some order cards directly from LC; others receive them from a commercial vendor; others photocopy LC proofslips; others photograph items in the National Union Catalog; and others (including most large and middle-sized libraries) order cataloging from a computer-based network such as OCLC, RLIN (Research Libraries Information Network), or WLN (Washington Library Network). In all these cases the ultimate source of most of the cataloging copy is the same--the Library of Congress.

There are cogent reasons for accepting LC cataloging. Its high standards of accuracy, reliability, and completeness are well known. Libraries have found that they can save a great deal of time and money by using LC cataloging copy and having a nonprofessional staff process it, instead of maintaining a staff of professional catalogers large enough to catalog everything originally. Thus it is not an exaggeration to say that--as far as cataloging is concerned--many libraries are in a state of dependence upon LC.

On January 1, 1981, LC will introduce a number of changes that will significantly affect every library that uses its cataloging. These changes were announced by LC in 1977. Since then they have been discussed at many library conferences and in many library publications.[1] In fact, the very day of transition (January 1, 1981) has become known as Day One.

Despite all the discussion, however, it seems that the true nature of the situation and its importance are often not understood by librarians, especially those outside the

1

area of technical services. The subject does have many intricate and esoteric aspects, and the articles and addresses which deal with it often presuppose a certain knowledge of and familiarity with the details of cataloging that many librarians do not possess. The unfortunate consequence has been a tendency for some librarians simply to dismiss the whole subject as something of concern only to catalogers or as something that only the mammoth research libraries need to worry about.

Nothing could be farther from the truth. The changes in LC cataloging will affect every library, large or small, that uses LC cataloging, and they will affect every person who uses the catalogs of those libraries. It would behoove all librarians--in fact, all serious researchers--to become familiar with this situation. That is the need which this work seeks to address. My intention is to present a clear, concise summary of the subject, which should be of interest to all persons who will be affected by the changes, from the librarian who is utterly unfamiliar with the <u>Anglo-American</u> <u>Cataloging</u> <u>Rules</u> to the librarian who is emersed in the details of cataloging codes and would like an opportunity to see the forest instead of the trees, to the researcher who is not a librarian but who uses the card catalog as an indispensable tool.

Part I (Areas of Conflict) and Part II (Resolving the Conflicts) should be of most interest to the general reader --the librarian or non-librarian who simply wishes to learn what is going to happen to the card catalog. Part III (In-House Strategies) deals with some of the technical aspects of the subject (in a condensed and simplified form) and is intended mainly for technical services librarians who are responsible for planning and directing actual operations. Part IV (A Longer View) briefly considers the larger rationale for and significance of the changes in LC cataloging.

I would like to thank Lynne Meyers, Coordinator of Network Services at Palinet, for reading the preliminary typescript and making valuable suggestions.

Areas of Conflict

Suppose that LC had the following books to catalog:
(1) a collection of letters by Mark Twain and (2) a report issued by the University of Chicago. If LC were cataloging these books before Day One (January 1, 1981), it would use the following forms of entry:

1) Clemens, Samuel Langhorne, 1835-1910.
2) Chicago. University.

And, indeed, when a person consults the card catalog of most libraries, he or she will find cards under the above entries.[2] If the user tries to look up the first under "Twain, Mark" or the second under "University of Chicago," he or she will most likely find cross-references to the forms of entry shown above.

If LC were to catalog these same books after Day One, however, it would use the following forms of entry:

1) Twain, Mark, 1835-1910.
2) University of Chicago.

AACR2 and Desuperimposition

The difference between the first pair of entry forms shown above and the second pair is a result of two actions which LC will take on Day One. It will adopt the second edition of the Anglo-American Cataloguing Rules (AACR2), and it will end its policy of superimposition (the policy of continuing to use established forms of entry). Although

AACR2 is the term most often used in library circles to refer to the changes in entry forms which will begin on Day One, the policy of desuperimposition (the ending of the policy of superimposition) is by far the more significant cause of these changes.

Most of the changes were actually stipulated, not just in the second, but even in the first edition of the Anglo-American Cataloging Rules (AACR1), which was published in 1967. When LC adopted this code, however, it maintained the policy of superimposition, which provided that forms of entry which had already been established would not be changed to conform to the new code. Thus LC continued to catalog books under "Clemens, Samuel Langhorne, 1835-1910" and "Chicago. University," and only new entries ("University of Zambia," for example) were established according to the new rules.

Now that the policy of superimposition will be abandoned on January 1, 1981, all changes specified in AACR2 will be reflected in the forms of entry on future LC cataloging. The consequence will be a large number of conflicts between pre-Day One forms of entry (now present on the cards already in most libraries' catalogs) and post-Day One forms of entry (which will appear on new cards). The conflicts fall into three major areas: personal authors, corporate authors, and series.

Personal Authors

When the old cataloging rules were in effect, LC established many authors under the full forms of their real names. As a result, library catalogs contain cards with headings like the following:

1) Clemens, Samuel Langhorne, 1835-1910.
2) Graham, William Franklin, 1918-
3) Lawrence, David Herbert, 1885-1930.
4) Mozart, Johan Chrysostom Wolfgang Amadeus, 1756-1791.

Starting January 1, 1981, LC will apply the rules of AACR2, which call for establishing the form of entry of an author under the name by which he or she is known. Consequently, when LC catalogs works by those authors cited above, it will use the following new forms of entry:

1) Twain, Mark, 1835-1910.
2) Graham, Billy, 1918-
3) Lawrence, D. H. (David Herbert), 1885-1930.

4) Mozart, Wolfgang Amadeus, 1756-1791.

Obviously, new cataloging with these forms of entry will conflict with the cataloging already in most libraries' card catalogs.

Corporate Bodies

In the past, LC entered many corporate bodies under place:

1) Chicago. University.
2) Indiana. Ball State University, Muncie.
3) New York (City). Museum of Modern Art.

These will now be entered under their actual names:

1) University of Chicago.
2) Ball State University.
3) Museum of Modern Art (New York, N.Y.)

If geographical designations are necessary (as in the last example) to differentiate bodies with common names, these designations will be added after the names.

In the past LC tended to enter corporate bodies as subordinate units of larger bodies:

1) Stanford University. Hoover Institution on War, Revolution, and Peace.
2) United States. Library of Congress.

Many of these will now be cataloged as direct entries under their own names:

1) Hoover Institution on War, Revolution, and Peace.
2) Library of Congress.

Series

Many series will be affected by the changes in corporate bodies. For example, in the past LC has traced a series issued by the University of Chicago in the following way:

Chicago. University. Modern philology monographs.

In the future such a series will be traced under its own name:

Modern philology monographs.

Subject Headings

Some discussions of the changes scheduled for Day One have added subject headings to the three categories mentioned above.[3] Subject headings, however, will not be affected by desuperimposition or by AACR2. In fact, they have already been undergoing radical changes over the past several years. LC does have some major changes planned, such as using the form of subject heading "World War, 1914-1918" instead of "European War, 1914-1918." But the rate of change may not even increase, simply because LC has already, over the past years, been making the changes it desires.

While subject headings are therefore not a part of the problem which this work addresses, they do serve as a useful analogy to the changes that will soon affect personal authors, corporate bodies, and series. As most librarians who have worked with the subjects section of the card catalog know, LC has canceled many established subject headings and has replaced them with more up-to-date terminology. "Hygiene, Public," for example, has been replaced by "Public health," and "Insurance, Social" has been replaced by "Social security."

Such changes have been widespread, and libraries have responded as their respective traditions and resources have dictated. Some, by means of extensive erasing and retyping, have kept the headings on their cards current with LC's newly adopted subject headings. Others have interfiled the old headings and the new headings, with an explanatory card placed at the front of the mixed sequence. Others have added see also references to link the old and new headings. Still others have merely placed a copy of the latest edition of Library of Congress Subject Headings in the vicinity of the public catalog and let the cards fall where they may.

Such has been the variety of responses to the changes in subject headings. In 1981 libraries will have to begin coping with changes in personal names, corporate bodies, and series. They will no doubt employ many of the techniques already developed in handling subject headings.

Resolving the Conflicts

Closing the Card Catalog

In 1977, when LC first publicized its decision to end superimposition and adopt AACR2, it also announced a third change scheduled for Day One--the closing of its card catalog and the beginning of a new, computer-based catalog. At the time, many libraries thought they would follow suit. A great deal of complaint was voiced about the shortcomings of card catalogs. They were charged with being costly to maintain, often misfiled, slow to update, and subject to physical deterioration. Much interest arose concerning alternatives to the card catalog. Although LC, at the urging of many libraries, postponed Day One from January 1, 1980, to January 1, 1981, it became obvious that the technology necessary for an on-line catalog would not be ready in time. Libraries began to consider COM (computer output microform) catalogs as a temporary alternative.

The idea, in its most common form, was for a library to obtain computer tapes, instead of cards, from OCLC. These tapes could be processed by a commercial vendor or perhaps by an in-house computer center in order to produce microfiche cards, which would serve as the library's public catalog. Several copies of the microfiche would be made and distributed throughout the library, and perhaps even outside it. They would be regularly replaced with updated microfiche, containing recent additions to the collection.

As libraries investigated the realities of this alternative to card catalogs, however, its initial attractiveness began to diminish. The principal factor seems to have been cost. COM catalogs are expensive--not merely to

7

set up, but also to maintain. Updating such a catalog involves not merely processing the new catalog records being added to the microfiche but also reprocessing all the records already on the microfiche, and vendor charges are usually based on the total number of records processed. Thus, even if a library's acquisitions remain the same each year, the cost of updating increases as the size of the catalog grows. Although COM would eliminate certain manual tasks (principally filing), it would also impose certain constraints. One would no longer be able to make adjustments for minor variations, as one can when filing cards. The entry forms would have to be perfectly uniform, or the machine would misfile them.

Two Catalogs

One less expensive alternative to a COM catalog would be a new card catalog. A library could close its old card catalog at the end of December, 1980, and start a new card catalog at the beginning of January, 1981, so that the old, pre-AACR2 forms of entry would remain in the old catalog, and the new, AACR2 cataloging with new forms of entry would form the new catalog.

But having two catalogs involves certain disadvantages, which will exist whether the new catalog is a card catalog or a COM catalog.

First, and most obvious, is the inconvenience to the user, who would be obliged to consult two separate catalogs. A special effort would have to be made by the library to make the user aware of the new catalog's existence and to justify its creation.

Second, and more fundamental, is the fact that simply closing the old catalog and starting a new one will not by itself solve the problem of conflicting entries. The new and old forms of the same entry will merely be located in different catalogs. Cataloging under "Clemens, Samuel Langhorne," for example, would remain in the old card catalog, while cataloging under "Twain, Mark" would appear in the COM catalog or in the new card catalog. It would then be necessary to develop some system of linkages (i. e. cross-references), so that a user consulting both old and new catalogs would be led to both the old and new forms of the same name.

Third, it will require a great deal of attention and effort to make sure that cataloging containing old forms of entry does not inadvertently slip into the COM catalog or into the new card catalog. LC has no problem in this respect, since all of its cataloging is prepared by its own

staff. It will simply instruct its staff to begin using
the new forms of entry on Day One, and all the cataloging
that goes into its new catalog will consequently contain
only the new forms.

The situation is more complex for other libraries,
since most of them use a combination of their own cataloging and cataloging from LC. It is the older LC cataloging
copy that presents a problem. Many libraries acquire older
books as well as new imprints. If cataloging for a book
had been done by LC before January 1, 1981, it might contain entry forms that conflict with AACR2 entries. A library using such cataloging copy would have to check the
entry forms and change them to the AACR2 forms. If it
failed to do so, it would soon find old forms of entry
cropping up in its new catalog.

This situation is further complicated by the actions of
the major on-line networks--OCLC, RLIN, and WLN, which together supply the cataloging for most of the large and
medium-sized libraries in the United States. In late
December, 1980, OCLC ran a computer program that converted
the old entry forms on the cataloging already in its data
base to the new entry forms. The conversion, however, was
not one hundred percent. As OCLC had anticipated, some of
the old entry forms were missed, and they will have to be
changed at a later date. Consequently a library using OCLC
to build a new catalog will still have to monitor the entries
of the cataloging it uses after Day One, to catch any uncon-
verted entry forms.

The same is true of RLIN and WLN, especially since these
networks do not have a program ready to convert their old
forms of entry to the new forms. As a matter of fact, on
Day One very little if anything will change in their data
bases, since it will be several weeks at least before the
new, AACR2 cataloging from LC finds its way onto computer
tapes and makes its appearance on libraries' computer ter-
minals. This would be a good reason for delaying the closing of the old catalog and the starting of a new one until
some time after January 1, 1981--specifically, until the
new cataloging from LC actually appears. But even after
that time the entry forms would have to be closely moni-
tored and many of them changed, since all the old cataloging in the RLIN and WLN data bases would continue to
display the old, pre-AACR2 forms.

To make things even more difficult, in many libraries
the persons who handle LC copy cataloging are nonprofes-
sionals. It is they who will have to differentiate between
old LC cataloging with pre-AACR2 forms of entry and new
LC cataloging with AACR2 forms, and it will probably also
be they who will have to change the old forms to the new

forms before ordering the catalog cards. While the on-line name authority file, which has been prepared by LC, would be of help in this task, it is no simple tool. Instead of showing a simple contrast between a single old entry form and a single new entry form, the name authority file contains a great deal of additional information that would confuse many professional catalogers, not to mention non-professionals.

Despite all these difficulties, a few libraries still intend to close their old card catalogs and set up a COM catalog or a new card catalog--perhaps as a preliminary step to going to an on-line catalog, or for reasons best known to themselves. But for the other libraries--the overwhelming majority--the future is clear. They will have to adjust their old card catalog to accomodate the new forms of entry. Most card catalogs probably will be replaced eventually by on-line catalogs, but that change may be a good many years away. Meanwhile, libraries will have to cope with a single card catalog as best they can, and that is the subject of the following section.[4]

Adjusting a Single Catalog

It is reasonable to assume that libraries will want, whenever possible, to change from the old forms of entry to the new. Certain libraries will, however, probably elect to do the reverse and maintain the old by changing the new. This alternative may be easier in the short run, but it may prove an unjustifiable burden in the long run. A library that changes the old to the new faces a task of finite duration, since once the old entries are changed, the job is over. But a library that decides to change the new to the old faces a task of infinite duration, since it will have to continue forever changing the LC cataloging it uses. The decisive factor is the degree to which a library depends on LC for its cataloging. If LC cataloging constitutes only a small percentage of the total, a library might well be justified in changing the few new entry forms it uses to match the old forms. In this case the library can still use the methods for making changes which are discussed below, simply by reversing the instructions to change the old to the new or to interfile the old under the new.

There are three major ways of coping with entry form changes: (1) erasing and retyping, (2) interfiling, (3) splitting the files.

1. Erasing and retyping, which is probably the most familiar method, simply involves physically erasing the old entry forms on the cards already in the catalog and typing

in the new forms. This is a laborious process, often with
messy results, but it is probably the best way to deal with
a change that involves only a few cards. (Obviously each
library will have to decide, on the basis of the size of
its catalog and work force, where "few" stops and "many"
or "too many" begins.) Most libraries, for example, probably have only a few cards under the entry "Graham, William Franklin, 1918-." In this case it will probably be
best simply to erase the "William Franklin" on these cards
and type in "Billy." After the cards are refiled in their
new place in the catalog, a cross-reference could be put
in the old place:

> Graham, William Franklin, 1918-
>   see
> Graham, Billy, 1918-

The cross-reference would be helpful, not only to the public using the catalog, but also to librarians. It would
assist the cataloger in gathering up a set of cards for
alteration or withdrawal, and it would prevent cards with
the old form of entry from inadvertently slipping into the
catalog.
   2. <u>Interfiling</u> can be used when there are too many
cards already in the catalog to erase the old headings. A
religious library might find that it has a great number of
cards under "Graham, William Franklin, 1918-." In this
case it could simply move the old cards to the place of
the new entry and put an explanatory card in front of them:

> Graham, Billy, 1918-
>   Cards with the following headings refer to the
>   same person and are filed together:
> Graham, Billy, 1918-
> Graham, William Franklin, 1918-

A cross-reference would be made from "Graham, William Franklin, 1918-" for the reasons mentioned above. In many cases
the new and old forms of the name would be so close together
that a cross-reference from the old form might be unneces-
sary. This will vary from library to library according to
the size of the collection. Some libraries would not need
to make a cross-reference from "Lawrence, David Herbert,
1885-1930" to "Lawrence, D. H. (David Herbert), 1885-1930."
But a cross-reference such as that from "Clemens, Samuel
Langhorne, 1835-1910" to "Twain, Mark, 1835-1910" would
obviously be necessary.
   3. <u>Splitting files</u> can be used when there are too many
cards to interfile easily. A large research library might

find that moving all the cards under "United States. Library of Congress" to "Library of Congress" would create a serious problem of overcrowding in the drawers of the card catalog. Instead, it could file the new cards under "Library of Congress" with a <u>see also</u> type card in front of them:

>   Library of Congress.
>   For other works issued by this body see
>   United States. Library of Congress.

The old cards already in the catalog would remain under the old form of entry, with a <u>see also</u> type card in front of them:

>   United States. Library of Congress.
>   For other works issued by this body see
>   Library of Congress.

Some libraries may establish specific criteria for using a specific method. For example, if there are more than a certain number of cards already in the catalog under an old entry form, the file would be split; if there are fewer cards than this number but more than a lower number, they would be interfiled; and if there are fewer than the lower number, they would be erased and retyped.

Note that in the examples of <u>see also</u> type references shown above, no indication of the date of change has been made. This is deliberate. Some libraries may consider making references specifically informing the user that "works cataloged before January 1, 1981," have been treated in one way and "works cataloged after January 1, 1981," have been treated in another. Such information is of no assistance to the user, who has little interest in when a book was cataloged. It may even mislead the user, who may mistakenly think that the notice refers to the dates when the books were <u>published</u>. In the same way, cross-references that refer to "works entered under the earlier (or later) form of the name" are of no assistance. How does the user know what is earlier and what is later? Moreover, adding "earlier" and "later" to a pair of <u>see also</u> type references for split files creates the possibility that they will be erroneously reversed by an inattentive or ignorant filer.

Many libraries may want to vary their selection of methods according to the type of entry involved as well as by the number of cards.

<u>Personal authors</u> are a highly used and hence a very important form of access to the library collection. For this reason a library might decide never to split the file

of a personal author but instead to use only interfiling or
erasing and retyping. The problem with splitting files is
that the user may overlook the <u>see</u> <u>also</u> directions at the
front of the file, even when they are on a raised card.

<u>Corporate</u> <u>bodies</u> can be handled by splitting files when
there are too many cards to erase and retype or when the
varying forms of the body are too awkward to interfile.
Corporate bodies often have sub-bodies added to their entry
forms, which make them tricky to interfile. As a form of
access, corporate bodies are far less often used than personal authors. Many library patrons are unaware of their
existence or are mystified by them. Again it is a question
of each library's function and priorities. A large academic library might consider the entry forms of universities
so important that it would want to interfile them all.
The result would be a great increase of cards under the
word "university," which might necessitate an addition of
new drawers at the end of the card catalog.

With regard to references, corporate bodies present
certain choices. Obviously when

    1) United States. Library of Congress.
    2) United States. Museum of History and Technology.

are changed to

    1) Library of Congress.
    2) Museum of History and Technology (U.S.)

a pair of <u>see</u> <u>also</u> type cards are needed for both bodies
if the files are split. But when

    1) Chicago. University. Department of Economics.
    2) Chicago. University. Department of Mathematics.

change to

    1) University of Chicago. Department of Economics.
    2) University of Chicago. Department of Mathematics.

probably a single pair of <u>see</u> <u>also</u> type cards would suffice,
one for "University of Chicago" and one for "Chicago. University."

<u>Series</u> are important to librarians for collection con-
trol, and therefore they may be handled in a special way.
The files could be split when the old entries are too nu-
merous to erase and retype, and a <u>see</u> <u>also</u> type reference
card could be placed at the front of the file of new entries:

> Modern philology monographs
>   For other works issued in this series see
> Chicago. University. Modern philology monographs.

The other <u>see also</u> type card would probably best be placed
<u>at the end</u> rather than at the front of the file of old en-
tries, at least for numbered series. That is where a user
would look for the higher numbers in the series, which
would be under the new form of entry:

> Chicago. University. Modern philology monographs.
>   For other works issued in this series see
> Modern philology monographs.

This procedure will not always result in a clean split. If
the series mentioned above were numbered, it would be ideal
to have numbers 1 through 23, for example, under the old
entry and numbers 24 and following under the new entry.
The two entry forms would be linked with <u>see also</u> type reference cards (as illustrated above), one after number 23
at the end of the old file and the other before number 24
at the front of the new file. But LC does not always catalog works in series in strict numerical order, nor do libraries always acquire them in that order. Consequently
the hypothetical series file mentioned above might actually
contain numbers 1-5, 8-11, 13-21, and 23 under the old form
of entry, and numbers 6-7, 12, 22, 24 and following under
the new form of entry. In this case it might be easier
simply to erase or cross out "Chicago. University." and
interfiles all the cards under the new entry with a single
cross-reference from the old entry form.
   It should be emphasized that the kinds of entry conflicts cited above under the general headings of personal
authors, corporate bodies, and series do not by any means
constitute an exhaustive list. They are only intended as
an indication of the major areas of change. Desuperimposition and AACR2 will bring about other alterations in entry forms, many too minor or too esoteric for most libraries
to worry about. The change in the form of conference names
is a case in point. Before Day One the entry was constructed
in the following order--name, number, place, date:

> 1) Louisiana Cancer Conference, 2d, New Orleans, 1958.
> 2) Symposium on Glaucoma, New Orleans, 1966.

After Day One such entries will be constructed in the following order--name, number, date, place:

> 1) Louisiana Cancer Conference (2nd : 1958 : New
>   Orleans)

2) Symposium on Glaucoma (1966 : New Orleans)

In most libraries the conference entries in the old form
are few enough and scattered enough simply to allow the
new conference entries to fall where they may in the card
catalog, without any adjustment.

No matter which entry conflicts a library regards as
important enough to resolve, they should all be amenable to
one of the three methods (erasing and retyping, interfiling,
and splitting files) outlined above, or to some modifica-
tion of these methods.

In-house Strategies

Size of the Change

Ever since LC announced in 1977 that it planned to end
superimposition and adopt AACR2, libraries have been at-
tempting to determine precisely how much of their card catalogs will be affected.[5] The usual method is to take a sam-
ple of the catalog and calculate (1) the percentage of entry
forms that will be changed if cataloged according to AACR2
and (2) the number of separate catalog records under these
forms. The resulting estimates have varied widely from
library to library, and it is no wonder. First, the changes
themselves are not always certain. In regard to many entry
forms, one will know whether or not they will change only
when LC makes its decision. Second, methods of making the
estimate vary. Does one count all the sub-bodies of a corporate entry form that will change or only the main body?
Third, the nature of library collections varies, and this
can influence the number of changes. A collection which
concentrates on literature, for example, rather than on
science, will tend to have more entries that will change
and more catalog records under each of these entries. The
forms of entry for classic literary authors tend to have
been established by LC at an early date, and literature
collections often feature large numbers of works and editions of works by these authors. Authors writing in the
field of science, by contrast, tend to be contemporary and
less prolific.

Not only do such estimates vary from library to library,
they also may not prove valid even for the very libraries
which made them. The simple calculation of how many of the

16

entries already in the catalog would be changed under AACR2
is only significant if a library actually intends to go
through the entire catalog and change all these entries.
Most libraries will have neither the desire nor the capa-
bility to undertake such a large and laborious task. Instead they will wait for the new entries on the new cataloging to appear and adjust the old entries as conflicts
arise. Many old entries will remain in their old form because the authors involved (personal or corporate) will not
produce new works or because the library will not happen
to acquire these works. Thus no conflicts will arise, and
no changes will be necessary. Consequently the number of
potential changes existing in the card catalog in the form
of obsolete entries will tend to be far greater than the
number of actual changes that will be required to resolve
actual conflicts.

If a library decides to make changes only when conflicts
appear, the crucial factor in determining the additional
work load will be, not the total number of changes, but the
rate of change--the number of conflicts appearing each day,
each week, or each month. This rate will vary significantly
according to the number of library acquisitions. The more
books a library acquires, the more frequently new forms of
entry on new cataloging will appear. For example, a small
library may feel that it has all the books it needs by Mark
Twain. Consequently it can allow the cards in its catalog
to remain under the entry "Clemens, Samuel Langhorne." But
an academic library is always acquiring new editions of
classic authors. Consequently, a few months or perhaps
weeks after January 1, 1981, it may receive a new book by
Mark Twain with new cataloging under the entry "Twain, Mark,"
and it will then have to make adjustments in the card catalog for all the old entries under "Clemens, Samuel Langhorne."

The rate of change will also be affected by which data
base a library uses to obtain its cataloging. OCLC has
converted the old entries in its data base to the new AACR2
forms, but RLIN and WLN have not. As a result, a library
which catalogs on OCLC will encounter more entries in their
new forms than if it were cataloging on RLIN or WLN.

Obviously one library's calculations as to the rate of
change it will encounter will be of little help to other
libraries with other kinds of collections and other acquisitions budgets. But one may hope that the rate of change
will be low enough to allow them to handle the additional
work without neglecting other important tasks or requesting
additional staff.

Identifying the New Forms of Entry

In order to resolve a conflict one must first be aware that it exists. Specifically, technical services staff must know when they are dealing with a form of entry on new cataloging that conflicts or may conflict with a form of entry already in the card catalog. This will not always be apparent, even to a professional cataloger, and the problem is compounded by the fact that in many libraries nonprofessional staff process the LC cataloging copy, which will contain the new entries. One might simply order the cataloging, wait until the actual cards arrive and are being filed in the catalog, and then resolve any conflicts that arise. But many conflicts will be difficult for filers to identify. If a filer were filing a card with the heading "Twain, Mark" and encountered a cross-reference pointing to "Clemens, Samuel Langhorne," he or she would realize that a conflict existed. But there are not always cross-references for the new entries to bump into. Most libraries probably have cross-references directing the user away from entries like "Twain, Mark" and "University of Chicago," but they may not have them under such lesser known entry forms as "Hoover Institution on War, Revolution, and Peace" or "Modern philology monographs." As a result, someone filing a card with either of these entries would not realize that the library had other cards under the forms "Stanford University. Hoover Institution on War, Revolution, and Peace" and "Chicago. University. Modern philology monographs."

Many libraries would therefore like to be able to identify conflicts or at least potential conflicts as a book is being cataloged. If a library is a member of an on-line network such as OCLC, RLIN, or WLN and consequently does its cataloging by means of a computer terminal, it will have certain advantages in identifying new entries. On-line systems of cataloging have become increasingly the rule in libraries over the past several years, and the rest of this section and the one that follows deal with them. Of the three major networks, WLN is limited to the northwest section of the country, and RLIN is generally limited to very large research libraries. OCLC has by far the largest membership, over 2000 libraries of all kinds and sizes. The following discussion will therefore concentrate on OCLC.

How can the person processing cataloging at a computer terminal know whether or not the entries on the cataloging are in AACR2 form? If they are, how can the person know what are the old forms of the entries they have replaced? In the case of OCLC's retrospective conversion of its data base, this will be relatively easy. OCLC has converted to their AACR2 form the entries on the cataloging already in

its data base.[6] The converted records carry distinctive
markings. A new, AACR2 form of entry is followed by a "≠w"
and an old form of entry, which has been replaced, appears
in an 87X field on the same cataloging record, with an ex-
act indication as to which line on the record has replaced
it. Thus, a catalog record which had a main entry "Clemens,
Samuel Langhorne" now contains two fields coded as follows:

>   100 10 Twain, Mark, ≠d 1835-1910. ≠w cn
>   870 19 ≠j 100/1 ≠a Clemens, Samuel Langhorne, ≠d
>   1835-1910.

The "100/1" in the 870 field indicates that the entry form
on this line was formerly in the 100 field.

This is perfectly adequate for the old, converted records, but what about new LC records which, after Day One,
will use the AACR2 forms of entry? One will be able to
recognize them by looking at the "Desc" subfield in the
fixed field at the top of a catalog record. If an "a"
appears here, then the entries on this record are in AACR2
form. In order to determine which old forms of entry (if
any) have been replaced by the new forms, one must make use
of the on-line name authority file, which is now available
on OCLC. For example, if a person finds a cataloging record
on the terminal with a "Desc: a" in the fixed field and
"Twain, Mark" as the main entry, he or she would then look
up the name in the name authority file. This would display
"Twain, Mark" in the 100 field, indicating that it is the
authorized form of entry for this author. Below the 100
field would be a number of 4XX fields, indicating other
forms of the author's name. Among these one could find
the form of entry that LC used before Day One by looking
for the letter "a" in the third place after the date num-
erals:

>   100 10 Twain, Mark, ≠d 1835-1910. ≠w n001790604aanann
>   400 10 Clemens, Samuel Langhorne, ≠d 1835-1910. ≠w
>   n011790604aaaana
>   ↑

Checking for Conflicts

Once those who do the cataloging are able to identify
the new forms of entry and the old forms they have replaced,
it will be necessary to establish a procedure for making the
appropriate alterations in the card catalog (erasing and retyping, interfiling, or splitting files).

If a library already has an established policy of check-

ing the forms of all entries against the catalog before
cards are actually ordered, then those who perform this
task could also check the catalog for old forms of entry,
as indicated by the 87X field or by the on-line name authority file. If a conflict is found, the person who finds it
could resolve it or could hand it over to the person or
subunit of technical services specifically designated to
perform the erasing and retyping, interfiling, or splitting
of files.

     If a library does not check entries before ordering
cards, the person at the terminal could make a note of the
potentially conflicting old and new forms of entry and pass
the information on to the appropriate individual or task
force, which would check the card catalog to determine if
there are any entries under the old forms and, if there are,
would resolve the conflicts between them and the new forms
of entry, which would appear on the catalog cards that had
just been ordered.

     In the process of checking for conflicts and resolving
them, a library would probably also want to adapt its own
in-house name and/or series authority files or to establish
a special authority file, in order to keep track of the
conflicts that had been resolved and how they had been resolved. By using such an authority file, a library would
be able to avoid continuing references to the public catalog to check for conflicts that had come up before and had
already been settled. Of course, if a library has a policy
of checking all entries in its public catalog, as mentioned
above, it would not be worthwhile to construct a special
authority file.

Old Forms of Entry on New Cards

     The above discussion has dealt with the problem of new
forms of entry conflicting with old forms already in the
card catalog. One should also be aware that not all cataloging processed after Day One will contain entries in the
new form, as indicated on pages 8-9. Of course, a library
could attempt to identify and convert all old entries to
their new forms before ordering cards, but it would probably
be easiest simply to allow cards with the old entry forms
to continue being added to the public catalog. One of the
advantages of interfiling and splitting files is that these
techniques of adjustment allow a catalog to continue re-
ceiving old forms of entry as well as new forms.

     The number of old forms which a library encounters in
its current cataloging will become progressively fewer and
fewer. OCLC users will have located and reported many old

forms of entry which the initial conversion of its data base missed. RLIN and WLN will make available to their members their own programs for conversion of old entries in their data bases. As the months and years pass, libraries will acquire fewer and fewer pre-1981 imprints with pre-AACR2 cataloging. Thus there will come a time when virtually one hundred percent of the cataloging processed by most libraries will contain only AACR2 entry forms. But for most libraries the process of transition will be a gradual one, with cataloging containing the new forms of entry gradually increasing and cataloging containing the old forms gradually diminishing. Only LC itself will experience a sudden and dramatic change.

A Longer View

Having considered the changes in LC cataloging and the degree to which they will affect libraries throughout the United States, one might well ask why these changes were necessary in the first place. Why could not LC have adopted AACR2 but retained the policy of superimposition? If it had done so, there would be no conflicts between forms of entry.

The most obvious answer is that the entry forms prescribed by AACR2 are those to which a user of the catalog would tend to go directly. When a person wants to find a book by Mark Twain or a publication by the University of Chicago, unless experience has taught him or her otherwise, he or she would probably look them up under "Twain, Mark" and "University of Chicago" rather than under "Clemens, Samuel Langhorne" and "Chicago. University." Consequently it would be an advantage to the user if all the entries in the card catalog were changed to the AACR2 form.

This consideration is unlikely to strike many librarians as adequate justification for the extra work the changes will create and the dislocations in the card catalog that will result. In fact, the true rationale lies elsewhere, in the realm of international cooperation in bibliographic control.

Almost everyone is aware of the enormous increase in publishing throughout the world. More is being published, and more of the publications are of interest to an international audience. Consequently there is a need for a system of international bibliographic control. LC may be able to handle American imprints (although one might argue that it could use some help from other libraries), but it cannot possibly maintain adequate control over foreign imprints.

The ideal system would be for countries to be able to rely on each other's cataloging, in the form of computer tapes produced by their respective national libraries--like the MARC (Machine Readable Cataloging) tapes produced by LC.

The first step toward such a system is an internationally accepted code of cataloging. This already exists for most of the English-speaking world in the form of the Anglo-American Cataloging Rules. But if genuine uniformity and compatibility is to exist in the cataloging of the countries that accept AACR, they must adhere to the rules and not insist on making exceptions in order to keep alive the practices established by their peculiar traditions of cataloging. International cooperation requires compromise, and compromise often involves giving up what a party views as familiar, easy, and therefore eminently reasonable--such as the retention of old forms of entry by superimposition.

Resistance and hostility to the changes in LC cataloging are entirely understandable. But since these changes are, at this point, inevitable, it would be best for libraries to consider the future benefits they may bring, as well as the present discomforts they are creating.

Notes

1. The literature is extensive. See, for example, the "Selected Bibliography on AACR2" in Doris Hargrett Clack, ed., The Making of a Code (Chicago: American Library Association, 1980), pp. 231-39.

2. Most of the specific examples of entry forms have been derived from the Library of Congress Cataloging Service Bulletin, nos. 6-10 (Fall 1979-Fall 1980).

3. For further discussion see Gregor A. Preston, "Coping with Subject Heading Changes," Library Resources & Technical Services 24, no. 1 (Winter 1980): 64-68.

4. For additional discussion see Joe A. Hewitt and David E. Gleim, "Adopting AACR2: the Case for Not Closing the Catalog," American Libraries 10, no. 3 (March 1979): 118-21.

5. Many libraries have published such in-house studies or summaries of them. See, for example Isabel Pang, "How AACR2 Will Affect a Medium-sized Library," The Journal of Academic Librarianship 6, no. 4 (September 1980): 208-9.

6. For details about OCLC's data base conversion, see OCLC Technical Bulletin, no. 97 (September 22, 1980) and RSTD Newsletter 5, no. 6 (November/December 1980): 69-70.

Bibliography

The following works discuss in detail some of the topics
which have been raised in the preceding pages.

Hoffman, Christa F. B., Getting Ready for AACR2: the Cataloger's Guide. White Plains, N.Y.: Knowledge Industry
Publications, 1980.

Kline, Peggy S. and Marion R. Taylor, "Adapting an Existing
Card Catalog to AACR2: a Feasibility Study," Library
Resources & Technical Services 24, no. 3 (Summer 1980):
209-13.

Malinconico, S. Michael and Paul Fasana, The Future of the
Catalog: the Library's Choices. White Plains, N.Y.:
Knowledge Industry Publications, 1979.

Potter, William Gray, "When Names Collide: Conflict in the
Catalog and AACR2," Library Resources & Technical Services 24, no. 1 (Winter 1980): 3-16.

Wiederkehr, Robert R. V., Alternatives for Future Library
Catalogs: a Cost Model. Rockville, Md.: King Research,
1980.